CW00739434

VICTORIA TO EAST CROYDON

Vic Mitchell and Keith Smith

First published April 1987
Reprinted January 1998

ISBN 0 906520 40 1

© *Middleton Press 1987*

Design - Deborah Goodridge

Published by
        Middleton Press
        Easebourne Lane
        Midhurst, West Sussex
        GU29 9AZ
Tel: 01730 813169
Fax: 01730 812601

Printed & bound by Biddles Ltd,
        Guildford and Kings Lynn

CONTENTS

MAPS & DIAGRAMS

GEOGRAPHICAL SETTING

The route leaves the lower Thames Valley and, on passing Clapham Junction, climbs onto the end of the low clay hills which arc from Wandsworth to Deptford, peaking to nearly 400ft. above sea level, near Crystal Palace. The line traverses the gravels of the gentle dip slope of the North Downs, reaching an altitude of 200ft. at East Croydon.

The Ordnance Survey maps reproduced in this album are to the scale of 25" to 1 mile, unless otherwise stated.

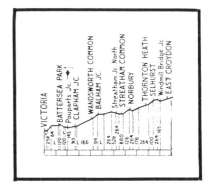

ACKNOWLEDGEMENTS

We are grateful for the assistance and advice received from many of the photographers mentioned in the captions and also from S.W. Baker, H.N. James and R. Randell. G. Croughton and N. Langridge have provided the excellent range of tickets and Mrs. E. Wallis has allowed us to use photographs taken by her late husband. The researchers of the Brighton Circle have been most helpful as have our wives, Mrs. E. Fisk and N. Stanyon.

HISTORICAL BACKGROUND

The London and Brighton Railway Company's route between London Bridge and Brighton was completed in 1841 but the line south as far as Redhill was shared with the South Eastern Railway. The L&B became the London Brighton & South Coast Railway in 1846 and in 1854 opened a branch to Crystal Palace, with the junction facing towards London Bridge. The Palace had been moved from Hyde Park after the Great Exhibition of 1851 and was to become a great tourist attraction, in open country south of London.

The West End of London & Crystal Palace Railway Co. was formed to build a line from a pier on the River Thames at Battersea to the Palace, where an end-on junction with the LBSCR would be made. The line was opened north to Wandsworth Common on 30th November 1856 and was extended to Battersea on 29th March 1858, the station being named Pimlico – a more select district on the north bank of the Thames. All trains were operated by the LBSCR and the route passed *under* the London & South Western main line, near Stewarts Lane, where a station was situated until 1st December 1858.

Another independent company with an

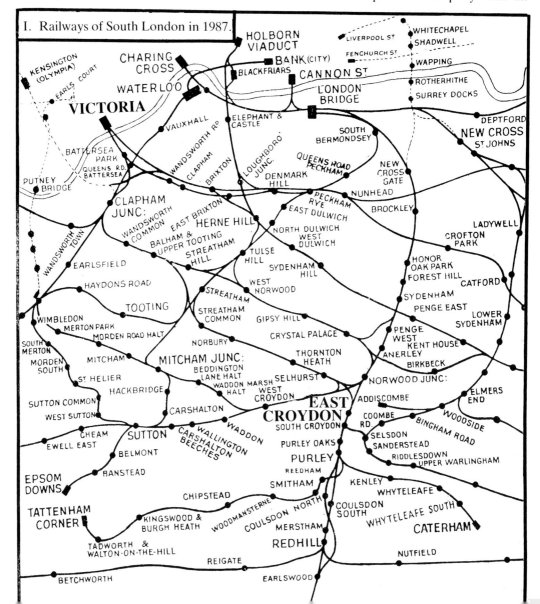

I. Railways of South London in 1987.

important part to play in the development of the route was the Victoria Station & Pimlico Railway Co., formed in 1858. It offered terminal facilities to the LNWR, the GWR, the LBSCR and the East Kent Railway (predecessor of the London, Chatham & Dover). The latter three companies became involved and whilst a single spacious station was planned, disputes brought about two separate stations with a dividing wall – the LCDR with the GWR on one side and the LBSCR on the other. The station came into use on 1st October 1860, although the roof was far from complete.

The more direct route from Croydon to Balham via Streatham Common was opened on 1st December 1862 with double track, a third one soon being added. Although the LBSCR and LSWR lines ran parallel in the vicinity of the present Clapham Junction, a station was not opened there until 2nd March 1863.

There was a 10mph speed limit through Stewarts Lane and a 1 in 53 gradient on a sharp curve up to the Grosvenor Bridge over the river. A new route, with more acceptable gradients and curves, and widening of the bridge was completed in 1867. The new lines passed *over* the LSWR's numerous tracks.

The first electric train services from Victoria commenced running on the South London line to London Bridge on 1st December 1909. These operated from overhead conductors at 6700 volts AC and this system was extended via Clapham Junction to Crystal Palace on 12th May 1911 and onto Selhurst in 1912. The wires were extended from Balham to Coulsdon North via Streatham Common and East Croydon, coming into traffic on 1st April 1925. All these routes were later converted to operate from conductor rails carrying 660 volts DC, the work being completed by the end of September 1929.

PASSENGER SERVICES

Details of the development of the high frequency local services have been well documented in other publications and so we confine ourselves to a few notes on unusual services. The main line trains using the route are described in our individual albums relating to the various Sussex lines converging on the route, but it is worth mentioning that many of these trains, in steam days, were divided at East Croydon, with separate portions for Victoria and London Bridge.

The gradual addition of a third track and eventually a fourth one, along the route, took place over a period of nearly 50 years. Combined with a fifth one over Grosvenor Bridge for empty carriages, these enabled the services to be increased in frequency whilst the number of routes converging at East Croydon also increased.

LNWR trains operated between Victoria and Willesden Junction from 2nd March 1863 until 1st October 1917, a journey which involved crossing the River Thames twice. The same company offered a service from the same date between East Croydon and Willesden Junction until WWII.

Other companies to use Victoria were the GER (to Liverpool Street until 1911); the

GWR (to Southall until 1915); the GNR (to Barnet via Blackfriars) and the Midland Railway to Finchley Road. All these services operated to and from the LCDR side of the station.

The SR provided an unusual service in the 1930's between Victoria and Poole, for the benefit of flying boat passengers. This necessitated the provision of a connecting line at Wimbledon.

Users of East Croydon station have had the benefit of a number of through trains to the Midlands and North of England. An early example was the 'Sunny South Express', which called each afternoon, in both directions, on the Liverpool/Manchester - Eastbourne service, from 1904. Apart from the war years, similar such services were available until the mid-1960s.

In 1979 Brighton - Manchester trains were reintroduced, these running via Kensington (Olympia), Reading and Birmingham. 1986 saw Newhaven Harbour as a new destination for trains from the North. 1987 is the date set for the commencement of electric services to Luton via Faringdon, bringing a long-lost useful cross-London link back into use.

VICTORIA

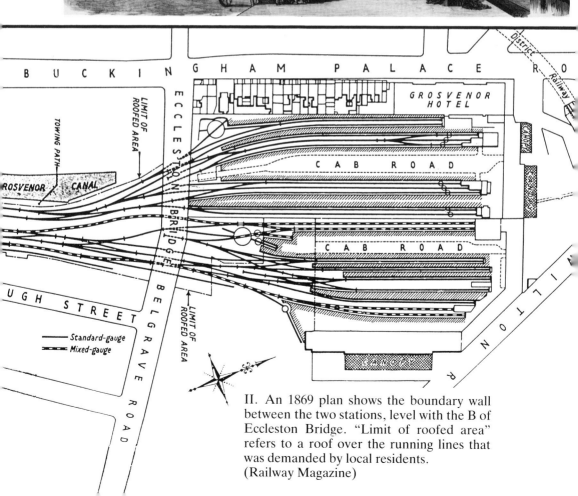

II. An 1869 plan shows the boundary wall
between the two stations, level with the B of
Eccleston Bridge. "Limit of roofed area"
refers to a roof over the running lines that
was demanded by local residents.
(Railway Magazine)

1. At the dawn of the railway age, most of the urban area of London was within a short walk of the City and so London Bridge was initially a satisfactory terminus for the LBSCR. The Great Exhibition of 1851 in Hyde Park and the opening of Victoria Street in August of that year stimulated rapid building development in what was to become known as the West End. Thus the late arrival of a station in 1860 was not marked with any ceremony – the first train simply leaving at 5.50am on 1st October. This engraving was produced in the following year. (National Railway Museum)

2. Whilst the train shed was quite imposing, the exterior was an unpretentious timber structure to which a cab roof or porte-cochère was added in 1880. It is seen beyond the horse-drawn omnibus. The advertisements in this picture and the next are worth studying with a magnifying glass.
(Lens of Sutton)

3. In the left background, the imposing Grosvenor Hotel towers above the adjacent terminus and on the right the booking office of the District Railway is clearly marked. A notice points to the alternative route to the Crystal Palace from the LCDR side of the station. The date is August 1888.
(E.R. Lacey collection)

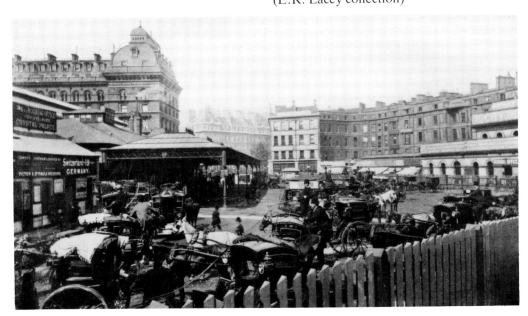

4. Eight platform faces were available in the LBSCR side of the station but these were eventually to prove inadequate as this part of London developed. The LCDR platforms were also used by broad gauge GWR trains until 1866 and are behind the wall on the right. (D. Cullum collection)

5. The LBSCR shared its side of the station with the LNWR, who operated a service to Willesden Junction from March 1863. The LBSCR's D class tank on the right looks well groomed with its polished buffers when compared with the saddle tank from north of the Thames. (National Railway Museum)

III. Lateral expansion was restricted, except where the remains of the Grosvenor Canal could be obliterated, and so it was decided to double the station *in length*. The layout employed enabled two trains to arrive in quick succession at one platform; the locomotive of the second train would uncouple; move forward; attach to the back of the first train and depart with it. The first locomotive would run round the second train; propel it into the north platform and then take it away. This unusual system worked well for many years. (Railway Magazine)

6. The Grosvenor Hotel and much of Victoria station had been built on the site of the Grosvenor Canal basin. In 1892, the purchase of land commenced to enable the station to be rebuilt and enlarged, a process that would take over 15 years. Suburban trains would be moved from the west side, as seen here, to the east, where they remain to this day.
(National Railway Museum)

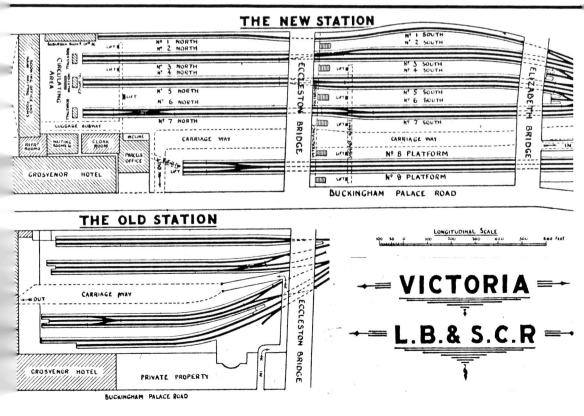

THE NEW STATION

CIRCULATING AREA

SUBURBAN BOOKING OFFICE &C

Nº 1 NORTH
Nº 2 NORTH

Nº 3 NORTH
Nº 4 NORTH

Nº 5 NORTH
Nº 6 NORTH

Nº 7 NORTH

LUGGAGE SUBWAY

CARRIAGE WAY

WAITING ROOMS &C

CLOAK ROOM

PARCELS OFFICE

INCLINE

GROSVENOR HOTEL

ECCLESTON BRIDGE

Nº 1 SOUTH
Nº 2 SOUTH

Nº 3 SOUTH
Nº 4 SOUTH

Nº 5 SOUTH
Nº 6 SOUTH

Nº 7 SOUTH

CARRIAGE WAY

Nº 8 PLATFORM

Nº 9 PLATFORM

ELIZABETH BRIDGE

BUCKINGHAM PALACE ROAD

THE OLD STATION

CARRIAGE WAY

OUT

GROSVENOR HOTEL

PRIVATE PROPERTY

ECCLESTON BRIDGE

BUCKINGHAM PALACE ROAD

LONGITUDINAL SCALE
100 50 0   100   200   300   400   500   600 feet

VICTORIA
L.B.& S.C.R

7. A photograph from about 1905 shows the south western part of the station under construction; Eccleston Road is behind the fence and the original stations are on the right. (British Rail)

→

8. On the left is the truncated Grosvenor Canal and in the centre is the new cab road, descending from the rebuilt Elizabeth Bridge. Less obvious are the roofs of the old station and a train running into it. (British Rail)

→

9. The exterior is nearing completion, in about 1907, and complements the Grosvenor Hotel, on the right. The porte-cochère was dismantled and part of it was re-erected at Hove, as shown in pictures 23 and 25 of our *Brighton to Worthing* album. (Lens of Sutton)

10. The new canopy had longer spans and therefore fewer stanchions. A subway under the station approach to the Metropolitan District Railway platforms was opened in 1878 and a bus station was built in the approach in 1926.
(National Railway Museum)

11. The platforms were numbered from the wall bounding the SECR station. (The SECR had been formed in 1899, by a managing committee of the LCDR and SER). The platforms were renumbered on 21st September 1925, to include both stations. The drum-like starting signals comprised a clear and an opaque glass, between which rotated a rectangular wire frame, covered with red fabric. The banner was electrically operated but illuminated by gas light, with an oil lamp in reserve.
(E. Jackson collection)

12. The postal and telegraph offices were important features of London termini. The public were able to use the railway telegraph system and pay an additional fee for the message to be delivered from the receiving station. Howells patent train indicator was provided until 1927, when it was replaced by a larger mechanical type.
(E. Jackson collection)

13. The overhead electrical equipment was suspended from the roof trusses and the luggage lifts on platforms 1 to 6 communicated with underground passages to the parcels office and the front of the station. W.H. Smith & Son have had a long association with the Brighton line and continue to occupy this prime position. The line of barriers was moved further south during alterations and further modernisation in 1985-86. (D. Cullum collection)

14. The electrification of the tramways of South London caused much loss of railway revenue and so suburban services had to be improved in speed and frequency. Here we see the answer. Most of the electrical equipment was from AEG in Germany – hence the reason for the abrupt cessation of LBSCR electrification during WWI, whilst LSWR schemes proceeded. Head code 1 indicated Crystal Palace. (E. Jackson collection)

15. A memorial to the 532 company's employees lost in WWI was dedicated and unveiled in 1921. A similar ceremony was held at Brighton. (British Rail)

16. An immaculate class H2 stands in front of the North Box, in about 1912. This box contained 83 electrical and 23 mechanical levers and controlled all the platform work. It was situated on platforms 5/6, close to Eccleston Bridge.
(F.M. Gates/D. Wallis collection)

17. South Box was at the end of platforms 7/8 and had a total of 269 levers. The track in the foreground had a then notable feature – a movable diamond crossing, which reduced the risk of derailment and gave a quieter and more comfortable ride. In the foreground is the Sykes drum-type ground signal, photographed between 1924 and 1929.
(D. Cullum collection)

18. The electro-mechanical system had many advantages, one of which was smaller lever frames. The signals were operated by electric motors driving a worm and wheel, and electric fouling bars indicated the position of trains on the instruments. A third box, Shunting Box, controlled the carriage sidings by means of 22 levers. (Lens of Sutton)

19. Ex-LSWR class L12 no.416 waits to depart for Bognor Regis in about 1935. The West Coast line had been electrified as far as West Worthing in 1933, the "juice" being available to Portsmouth and the branches in 1938. (C.R.L. Coles)

20. The intricate and ingenious electro-mechanical signalling, with its numerous signal boxes, was abandoned on 4th June 1939, in favour of an all electric system with miniature levers. The new box controlled colour light signals as far as Battersea Park, the route including two double tracks and a revsible carriage road. The box became redundant on 1st May 1984 when the Victoria Signalling Centre at Clapham Junction took over its work. This centre now controls all movements south to Norbury. (British Rail)

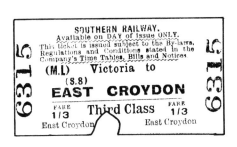

SOUTHERN RAILWAY.
Available on DAY of issue ONLY.
This ticket is issued subject to the By-laws, Regulations and Conditions stated in the Company's Time Tables, Bills and Notices

6315 / 6315

(M.L) Victoria to
(S.8)
EAST CROYDON
FARE 1/3   **Third Class**   FARE 1/3
East Croydon   East Croydon

21. The new signal box (on the right) received the blast from a bomb which destroyed all the Central Division running lines on 21st December 1940. No glass remains in the building behind and the lighting standard was blown down onto the turntable.
(British Rail)

22. A wall of sandbags had been built on 13th May 1941 to protect the station and the Army vehicles, in case the bomb exploded whilst it was being de-fused. A graphic account of the SR during WWII is told in *War on the Line*, now reprinted by Middleton Press. (British Rail)

23. A delayed action bomb exploded the same day, after a three day wait, damaging wagons brought in earlier to remove debris from a previous raid. (British Rail)

24. Many who remember the pre-television era will have memories of the NEWS THEATRE. That at Victoria opened on 11th September 1933 and showed short repeated films of recent news events (only a few days old), often interwoven with brief cartoon films. This 1949 picture shows that the departure indicator included services on the former SECR routes, the archway to that side of the station having been cut through the dividing wall in 1924. (British Rail)

25. The "Brighton Belle" brought a change from the uniform green trains that dominated the station for so many years. Three five-coach sets were in use until 30th April 1972, although initially they continued to use the famous name "Southern Belle". (C.R.L. Coles)

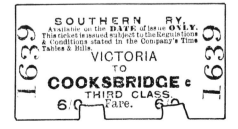

1639 SOUTHERN RY.
Available on the DATE of issue ONLY.
This ticket is issued subject to the Regulations
& Conditions stated in the Company's Time
Tables & Bills.
VICTORIA
TO
COOKSBRIDGE c
THIRD CLASS.
6/0 Fare. 6/0
1639

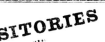

26. The 10.25am Newhaven Boat Train is seen climbing the 1 in 64 gradient on 5th August 1956 behind class H2 no.32425 *Trevose Head*. At this time steam on the Central Division from Victoria was otherwise restricted to a few secondary routes. (S.C. Nash)

27. Younger readers will need to know that BOAC stood for British Overseas Airways Corporation, although its passengers had little to do with Victoria station and were mainly taken by bus to Heathrow. British United Airways opened terminal facilities over platforms 15/16 on 1st May 1962 in connection with their Gatwick services. This led to a scheme in 1980 to build the massive concrete raft which now almost hides the trains. Here unit no.5775 departs for London Bridge on 11th August 1970. (J. Scrace)

28. Looking south against the sky, there are the four chimneys of the now redundant Battersea Power Station, the Battersea gas holders and the chimney of the sewage pumps. The main interception sewer runs from the waterworks-like building, behind the trees, to Beckton in East London. The 'Chatham' lines pass under the tapered part of Ebury Bridge and on the right of the 'Brighton' lines are nine carriage sidings. (British Rail)

GROSVENOR ROAD

29. Grosvenor Road station was opened as a ticket collecting platform in 1867 and a normal station on 1st November 1870, closing completely on 1st April 1907. This northward view was taken from the down local platform just prior to the completion of electrification in 1909. (R.F. Resch collection)

30. The Grosvenor Bridge was known as Victoria Bridge in its early years and was designed by John Fowler. The four wrought iron spans of 176ft length gave a 22ft headroom at high tide and extensive reconstruction took place in 1963-68. "Brighton Belle" crosses the graceful structure in February 1972. (J. Scrace)

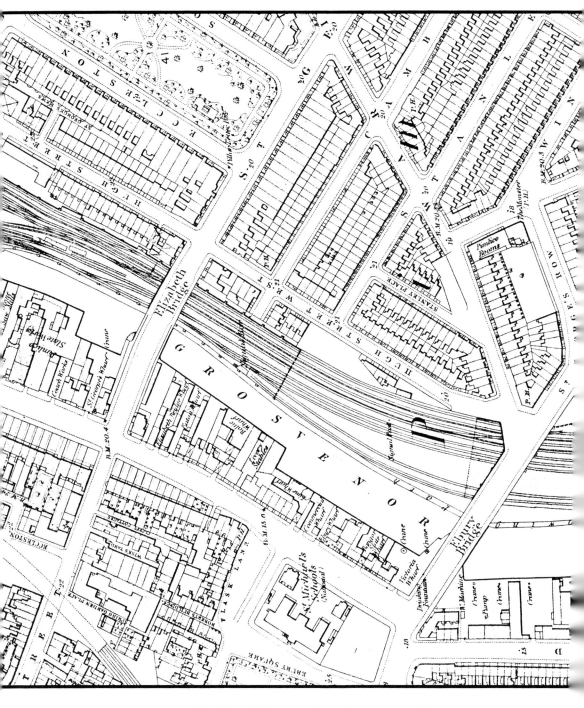

IV. The 1869 map shows the extent of the
Grosvenor Canal before the expansion of the
station, the uses of the wharves being worthy
of study. The LBSCR had three tracks on the
bridge at this time and the station at Grosvenor Road is shown.

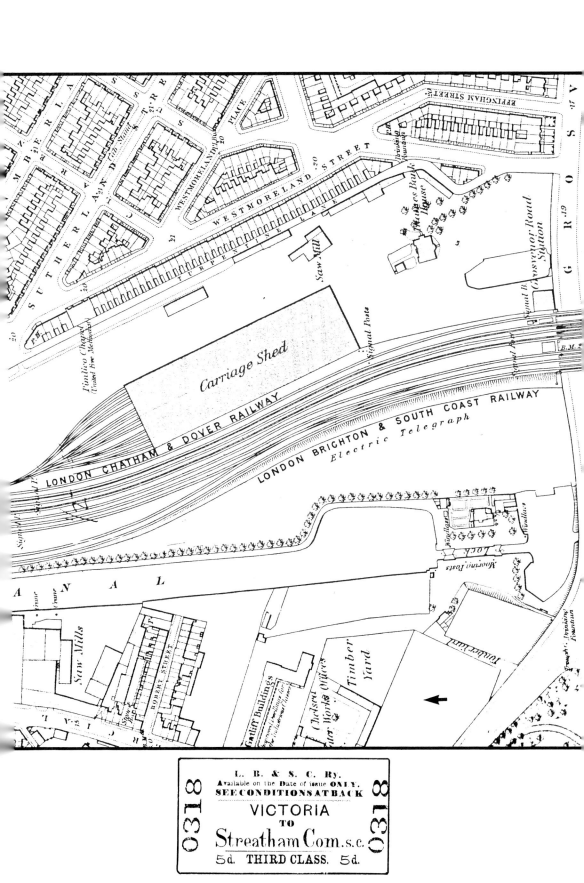

Carriage Shed

LONDON CHATHAM & DOVER RAILWAY

LONDON BRIGHTON & SOUTH COAST RAILWAY

Electric Telegraph

Westmoreland Street

Effingham Street

Grosvenor Road Station

Saw Mill

Saw Mills

Robert Street

Timber Yard

Timber Yard

Gatliff Buildings

Chelsea Water Works Offices

Mooring Posts

Lock

Findico Chapel

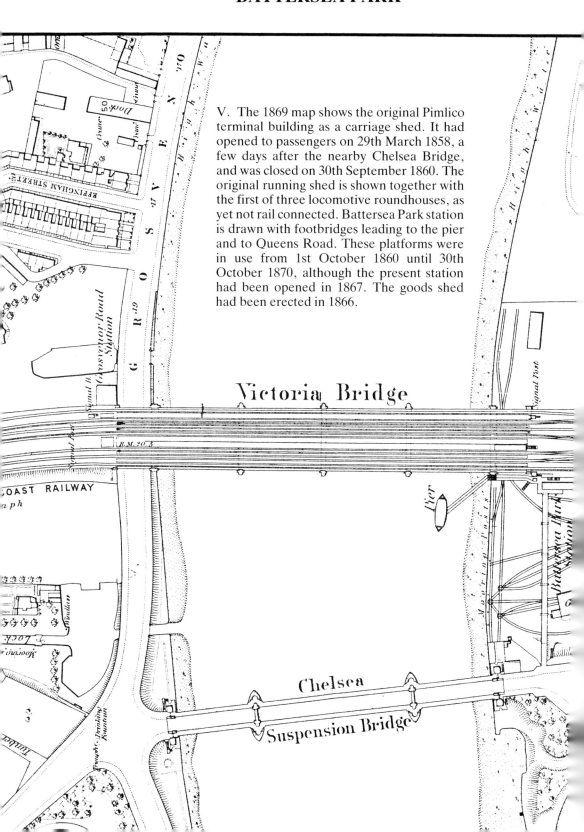

V. The 1869 map shows the original Pimlico terminal building as a carriage shed. It had opened to passengers on 29th March 1858, a few days after the nearby Chelsea Bridge, and was closed on 30th September 1860. The original running shed is shown together with the first of three locomotive roundhouses, as yet not rail connected. Battersea Park station is drawn with footbridges leading to the pier and to Queens Road. These platforms were in use from 1st October 1860 until 30th October 1870, although the present station had been opened in 1867. The goods shed had been erected in 1866.

Victoria Bridge

Chelsea

Suspension Bridge

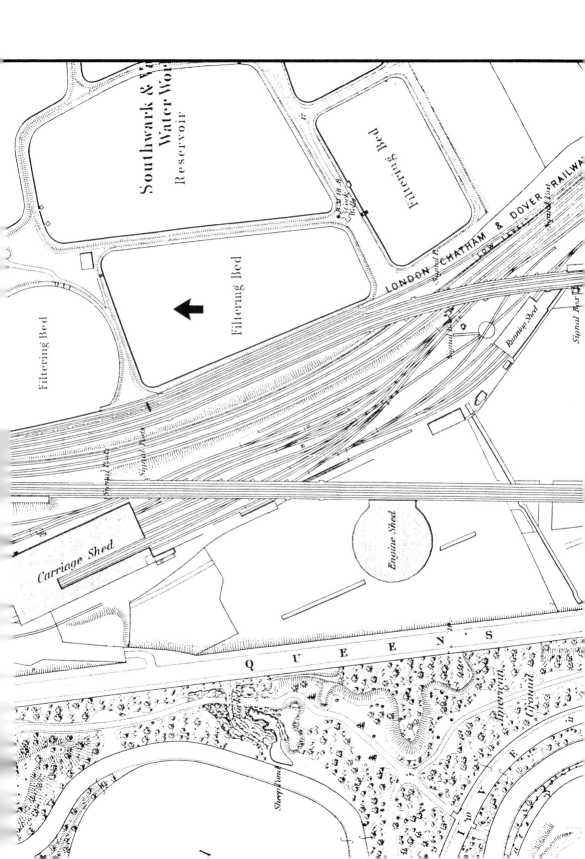

Southwark & V…
Water Wo…
Reservoir

Filtering Bed

Filtering Bed

Filtering Bed

LONDON CHATHAM & DOVER RAILWA…

Running Shed

Signal Box

Carriage Shed

Engine Shed

Q U E E N ' S

Sheep Pond

American Ground

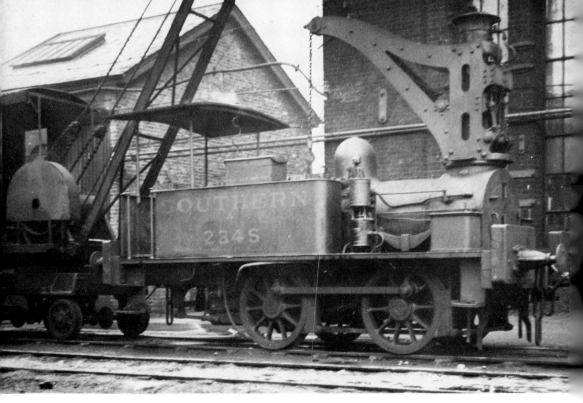

31. Looking north towards the goods depot in 1911, it is not clear that many of the lines serving it passed under the 1867 high-level tracks. Two of the roundhouses were this side of the elevated route and were linked under it to the third one. The former contained 55ft turntables and the latter had one of 45ft length. (Lens of Sutton)

London Brighton and South Coast Railway.

East Grinstead to

Battersea P.

32. Most of the engines were transferred to the former LCDR Stewarts Lane shed after the electrification of the main line in 1933. One interesting and unusual machine was photographed in May 1938. It is ex-SECR no.302, capable of lifting 50cwt and built by Neilsons in 1881. (J.G. Sturt)

33. The original low-level lines remain in use today but mainly for empty stock movements. They were electrified at the time of the Kent Coast electrification scheme. This northward view is from the ex-LSWR main line bridge on 24th April 1957 and it shows the original LBSCR route under the camera with a left fork going to Battersea Pier. On the right is the double track of the early low-level LCDR route to Victoria. The train is crossing to it from the former Battersea Pier line. (P. Hay)

34. Here we look towards Victoria on 4th May 1961, under Battersea Park Junction box which controlled the divergence of the South London line to London Bridge. The staff crossing in the foreground had no safety gaps in the conductor rail and has been abolished. The signal box closed on 7th October 1979. (British Rail)

35. Looking in the opposite direction, from the signal box on the same day, we see the South London line curving away on the left and the local lines to and from Clapham Junction underneath us. The up main line has no platform here, as it was laid in 1903, long after the station was opened. (British Rail)

36. The exterior was photographed in 1978, in the afternoon shadow of the former LBSCR bridge. The elegant facade and ornate booking hall were splendidly restored in 1986 and justify breaking one's journey to Victoria to inspect them. (J. Scrace)

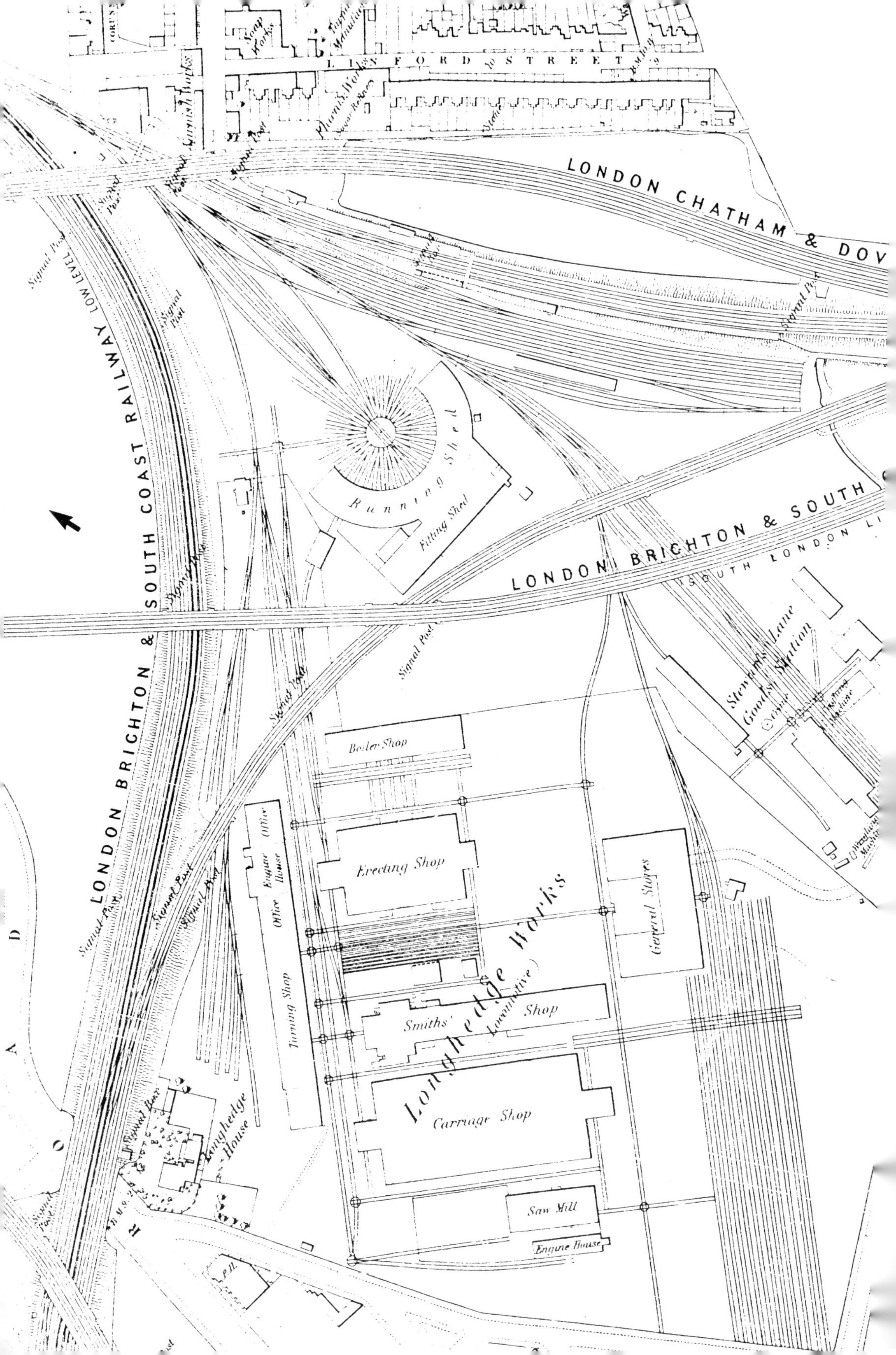

LIN FORD STREET

LONDON CHATHAM & DOV

LONDON BRIGHTON & SOUTH

SOUTH LONDON LI

LONDON BRIGHTON & SOUTH COAST RAILWAY

LOW LEVEL

Running Shed

Fitting Shed

Stewart's Lane
Goods Station

Boiler Shop

Engine
Office

Office
House

Erecting Shop

General Stores

Turning Shop

Smiths' Shop

(Locomotive) Shop

Longhedge Works

Carriage Shop

Longhedge
House

Saw Mill

Engine House

VI. The LSWR main line runs parallel to the left margin of this 1869 map. Although it primarily shows the LCDR locomotive works (before it was moved to Ashford), it also shows the LBSCR low-level route; part of the high-level (bottom left) and the connection to the LCDR passing under the South London Line. Compare this with map X, of 1916, in our *Waterloo to Woking* album.

37. Pouparts Junction is where the low-level and high-level lines to Victoria diverge. In 1986 the low-level route was still used by an occasional passenger train, such as the up morning boat train from Newhaven. This view of the grimy box was taken in 1933. (Late E. Wallis)

38. Headcode 16 was for Littlehampton but in 1933 it indicated West Worthing, then the limit of the conductor rail. The rear of this train is traversing Pouparts Junction, the box being visible on the right. The other train is on the down main line from Waterloo, which later became the up local. (Late E. Wallis)

CLAPHAM JUNCTION

39. Limited clearances between the LBSCR and LSWR tracks necessitated provision of these ugly cantilevered structures which extended, wireless, over the fast lines. The railway was built on part of Mr. Poupart's market garden – the family's famous jam was later produced in Twickenham.
(D. Cullum collection)

VII. Clapham Junction area development diagram. (Railway Magazine)

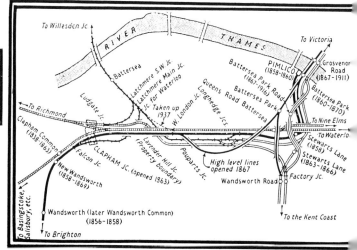

40. Looking north from St. John's Hill Bridge we see the 1838 double track of the LSWR on the left; the 1858 triple track of the LBSCR in the centre and the mixed gauge tracks of the West London Railway on the right. The latter enabled 7ft gauge trains of the GWR to terminate here.
(National Railway Museum)

41. Two up and one down line sufficed until quadrupling was completed in the early years of this century. The station was opened on the same day as the West London line to Kensington (1st March 1863) and at last it was possible for passengers to change between the LSWR and LBSCR systems.
(D. Cullum collection)

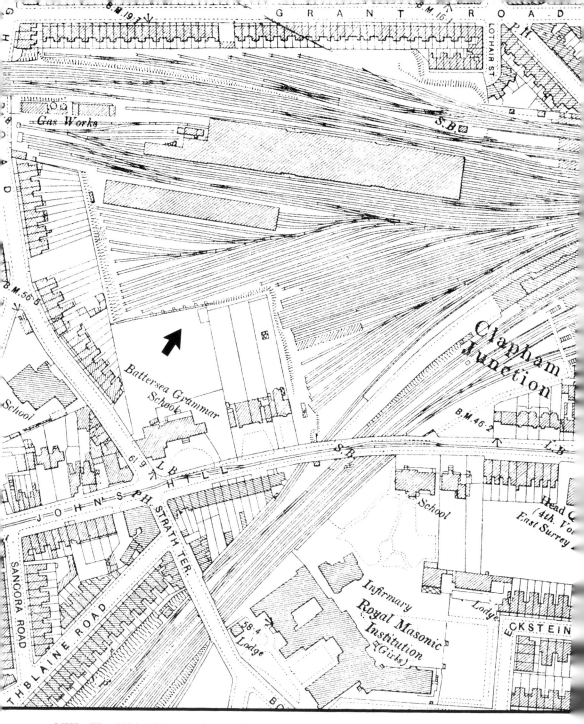

VIII. The 1894 edition makes an interesting comparison with the 1916 one, shown as map XIII in the *Waterloo to Woking* album. The West London line is seen above the LNWR Falcon Lane Goods Depot and the Victoria and Waterloo lines are above that. The LSWR and LBSCR main lines are at the bottom of the map, whilst the Windsor lines are at the top left. Note the numerous passing loops on the tram tracks.

42. South Box, seen towering above St. John's Hill bridge, was erected upon completion of the fourth track to Streatham Junction in 1897 and was later known as C Box. The LSWR main line, on the right, is still only double track in this view. (Lens of Sutton)

43. The LBSCR presented a fine frontage to St. John's Hill with an entrance from the pavement and a cab road at a higher level on the west side. Note the tramway conduit, used in preference to overhead wires. 1987 saw the construction of a fresh booking hall in a new shopping complex and access to the platforms, once again, by means of the subway. (Lens of Sutton)

44. The down local starting signals were so tall that they could be obscured in fog and so these miniature repeaters were provided at the base of the post. Illumination was by the well shaded gas light. (Late E. Wallis)

46. A derailment under the wires in 1916 caused a problem now familiar north of London – the impossibility of raising a breakdown crane jib amid the aerial structures. Observe the high average age of the labourers – younger men were in France fighting for King and country at that time.
(National Railway Museum)

45. On the right is a temporary signal box which stood over two of the LSWR Windsor lines in about 1906-12 and on the left are the buffer stops of the transfer siding between the LSWR and the LBSCR. Such vehicles as horse boxes and milk vans would be placed in this siding for retrieval by the other company's engine. (Late E. Wallis collection)

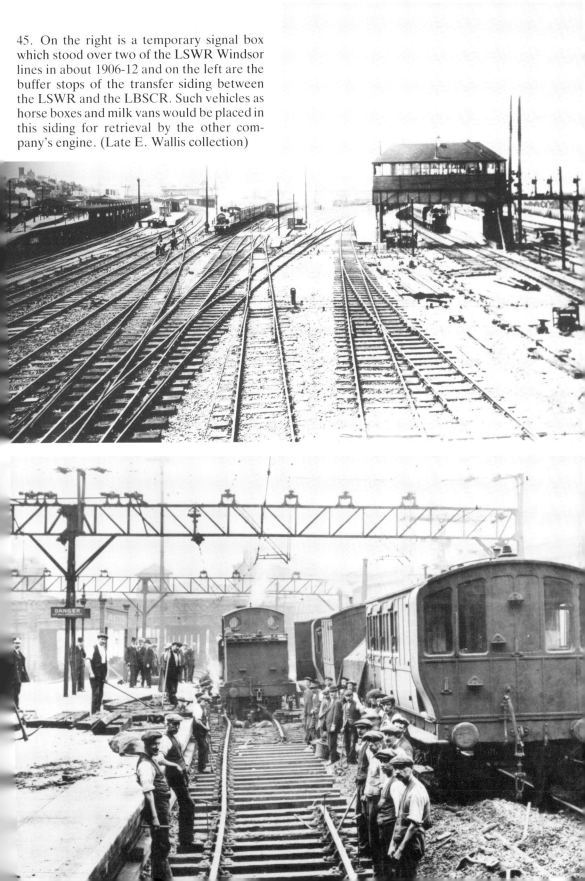

47. "Gladstone" class B1 no. B190 passes through on the "down main" on 25th July 1926. The prefix 'B' was added in 1924 by SR to all ex-LBSCR locomotives to distinguish them from those of Ashford or Eastleigh origin. (H.C. Casserley)

48. The unusual panorama from the top of the down local starting signals in 1928, emphasises the massive dimensions of the combined luggage and footbridge, erected by the LBSCR in the first years of the century. The catenary gantries sprout through the roofs and span platforms 12 to 15 (present numbers), whilst in the left distance the Windsor line platforms are visible. (Late E. Wallis)

49. Platforms 17 and 18 serve the West London Line and LMS 2–4–2T no. 2510 is seen leaving no. 17 (then no. 11) on 17th March 1928, with an East Croydon to Willesden Junction service. The leading vehicle is a horse box in which a compartment is provided for the groom and the locomotive still displays its LNWR number plate.
(H.C. Casserley)

50. Looking up from platform 12 in 1957, as a down milk train is about to pass under the 'A' Box, which was East Box until 1924. On the right is 'B' Box which controlled the 'Brighton lines' in the area from 12th October 1952 until 17th May 1980. On the extreme right, the West London lines drop away, past Pig Hill sidings. (British Rail)

51. The first of three photographs taken on 21st September 1952 reveals the clashing styles of construction employed by the two companies. On the left is part of the former LSWR footbridge which connected direct to St. John's Hill until WWII and was later converted into a staff training school. The West London lines on the right received conductor rails in 1968 so that the platforms can be used to terminate trains from the south in an emergency. (D. Cullum)

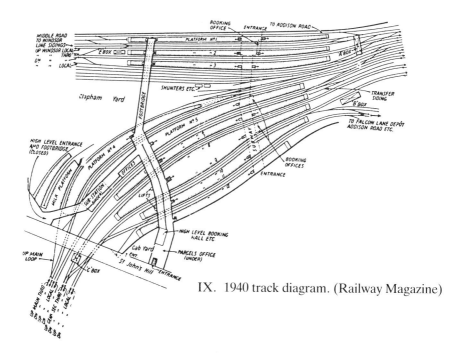

IX. 1940 track diagram. (Railway Magazine)

52. 'C' Box was known as South Box in LBSCR days and its functions were transferred to the new 'B' Box on 12th October 1952. The boundary between Central Division and Western Division is marked by the white cable troughing. (D. Cullum)

53. Moving further south, we see the roof of 'C' Box beyond the signals and a Victoria to Beckenham Junction train curving away from the Waterloo lines. The LSWR's first station was situated in the cutting on the left, from 1838 to 1863, and the LBSCR's New Wandsworth station was south of Battersea Rise bridge, from which this picture was taken. (D. Cullum)

NEW WANDSWORTH

54. A K class 2–6–0 toils south in 1933, passing the New Wandsworth goods yard which was largely at a higher level than the main line. The overhead wires had gone by then and some of the gantries were used for other purposes, such as the construction of Ryde locomotive shed. The lower signals were repeaters for the upper ones and the single distant arm was for the West London route. (Late E. Wallis)

X. New Wandsworth station closed to passengers on 1st November 1869 but, as this 1916 map shows, the goods yard was retained in use, eventually closing in 1964. The signal box was taken out of use in 1952.

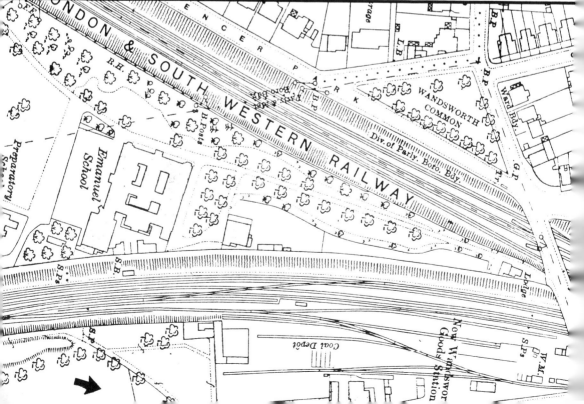

WANDSWORTH COMMON

55. The wide open countryside was beginning to be developed with high class housing in the 1860s and the New Wandsworth station was becoming increasingly dilapidated. It was therefore decided to build a new station on Wandsworth Common, which came into use on 1st November 1869. (Lens of Sutton)

56. Spacious platforms with wide flower borders and extensive canopies were deemed appropriate for this superior suburb. The main buildings are on the present down local platform. (Lens of Sutton)

57. A southbound train hauled by class E5 0–6–2T no. 590 passes under Nightingale Lane bridge in about 1915. The limited clearances under many bridges necessitated the provision of dead lengths of conductor wire under them. (R.F. Resch collection)

58. A view south from the footbridge in March 1928 shows the position of the 1897 signal box and the final arrangement of overhead electric power cars, which were locomotives in all but name. A similar system was tried 50 years later in BR's Advanced Passenger Train. (H.C. Casserley)

XI. 1894 – triple track, with the signal box astride one of them.

59. The universal use of coal for domestic heating generated considerable rail traffic both here and at the nearby New Wandsworth coal yard. The copper conductor was suspended from *two* stranded galvanised wires, coated in tar. The 6-car stop position is marked on the lamp glass. (Late E. Wallis)

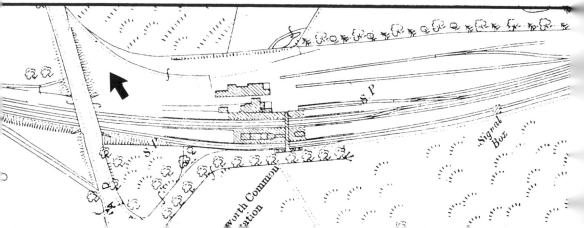

XII. 1916 – quadruple track.

60. The down home signals were supported by the massive tapered wooden posts much favoured by the LBSCR. The North Box is visible in this 1930 view. It was built to provide an additional block post to allow for increased traffic in World War I, but it was never brought into use. (Late E. Wallis)

61. Looking south from the road bridge in September 1952, we witness the signalling in transition. The catenary gantry was inexplicably still standing over 10 years later. Only a small portion of the canopy over the up main platform has been retained, near the entrance. (D. Cullum)

62. Class C2X no. 32451 plods along the down local line in July 1956. Such scenes would not last much longer – the goods yard here closed in 1964. (P. Hay)

BALHAM

63. The station opened on 1st December 1856, the same day as the line between Crystal Palace and Wandsworth. It was soon rebuilt, in readiness for a third track which came into use on 1st September 1863. A second look may be needed to see that the COCOA advertisement is on the modesty board of a LCC tramcar. (Lens of Sutton)

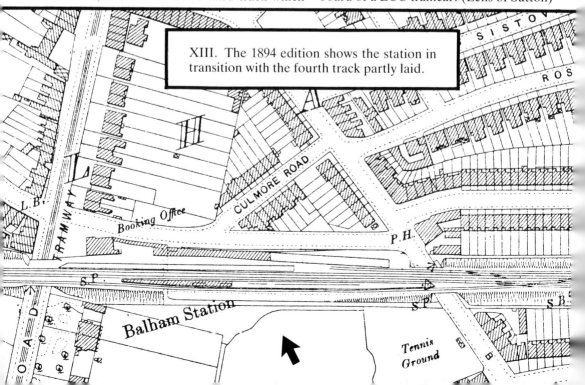

XIII. The 1894 edition shows the station in transition with the fourth track partly laid.

64. Looking towards the junction before the next rebuilding, we see WH Smith & Son advertising their now long-forgotten library service, which was once an important part of their empire. (Lens of Sutton)

65. The bridge over Balham High Road is seen on 21st September 1952 with one colour light signal in position, ready to displace the semaphores. (D. Cullum)

66. A photograph from the other end of the station on the same day shows the original Crystal Palace route running straight into the distance and the more direct route to Croydon, that we shall follow, turning right between the old and new signal boxes.
(D. Cullum)

London Brighton & South Coast Railway.

Littlehampton to

Balham

67. The shabby station, seen here in March 1954, was rebuilt yet again. A gas lamp stands on this platform, opposite a concrete standard waiting for the new electric lights. (D. Cullum)

68. Six months later, a picture from the same viewpoint reveals a major transformation taking place, the greatest benefit of which was a wider and safer island platform. The down local line no longer had two platform faces – always an operational problem. (Pamlin Prints)

69. Wiring was very labour intensive and also dangerous – no wonder safety rules were introduced. Balham Junction Box is in the background. (D. Cullum collection)

70. The new Balham box came into use on 12th October 1952 and was situated in the V of the junction. It was superseded by the Victoria Signalling Centre on 7th June 1981. (J. Scrace)

71. Balham Intermediate Box is on the down side, in the distance, close to Tooting Bec. The locomotive is 2–2–2 no. 329 *Stephenson* and the leading coach is a 'Pullman Pup' containing a generator which provided the new 'electrical illumination' to the three Pullmans which follow it. (D. Cullum collection)

72. The LBSCR introduced the 'Motor Train' in the early years of this century, for lightly loaded services. This example is a 'Balloon' coach, propelled by a Terrier 0–6–0T, which is hauling a six-wheeled brake third. (D.E. Wallis collection)

74. The fourth picture at this popular photographic location was taken on 28th September 1912 and shows class B2X no. 322 hauling a horse box and four gas tank wagons to Eardley carriage sidings. The gas was used for carriage lighting and Pullman car cookers. (K. Nunn/LCGB)

73. The first national railway strike took place on 18th and 19th August 1911. As the railway companies were in fear of their vital equipment being damaged, police and military protection was requested. Such an unusual assignment seems to have demanded a compromise uniform – battledress below the chin and ceremonial above. (Lens of Sutton)

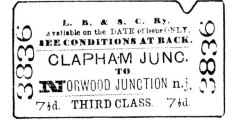

L. B. & S. C. Ry.
Available on the DATE of issue ONLY.
SEE CONDITIONS AT BACK.
CLAPHAM JUNCTION
No.2   TO
Grosvenor Rd G:rd.
2d.   THIRD CLASS.   2d.
15144

(No. 4)   (No. 4)
2nd - SINGLE   SINGLE - 2nd
Clapham Junction to
Clapham Junction   Clapham Junction
Thornton   Crystal
Heath, etc.   Palace, etc.
CRYSTAL PALACE, GIPSY HILL or
THORNTON HEATH
(S)   1/9   Fare   1/9   (S)
For conditions see over   For conditions see over
9168

75. The proximity of Buckingham Palace to Victoria station has made it the starting point for most Royal rail journeys in the south. One such annual trip has been to Tattenham Corner, for Epsom Races. "Schools" class no. 30926 *Repton* approaches Streatham Common on 6th June 1962. (J. Scrace)

→

XIV. The 1898 map has the Victoria to Croydon line from top to bottom and the Sutton to London Bridge line from left to right. A short siding is shown, this being used for coal to the waterworks pumps.

L. B. & S. C. & L. & N. W. Rys.
Available on the DATE of issue ONLY
STREATHAM HILL TO   BERKHAMSTED
Via Clapham Junc. & Kensington or Via Victoria
& Kensington by L. & N. W. or District Rys.
or Via London & Euston.
2s. 6¼d.   THIRD CLASS.   2s. 6¼d.
The connection of trains not guaranteed.
Not Transferable.   Issued subject to the
Conditions in the Time Tables of the respective
Co's over whose lines this ticket is available.
BERKHAMSTED
0163

SOUTHERN RY.
Available on Day of issue ONLY.
This ticket is issued subject to the By-Laws
Regulations & Conditions stated in the
Company's Time Tables, Bills & Notices.
STREATHAM COMMON
TO
WANDSWORTH COM.
THIRD CLASS
4d.   Fare   4d.
4363

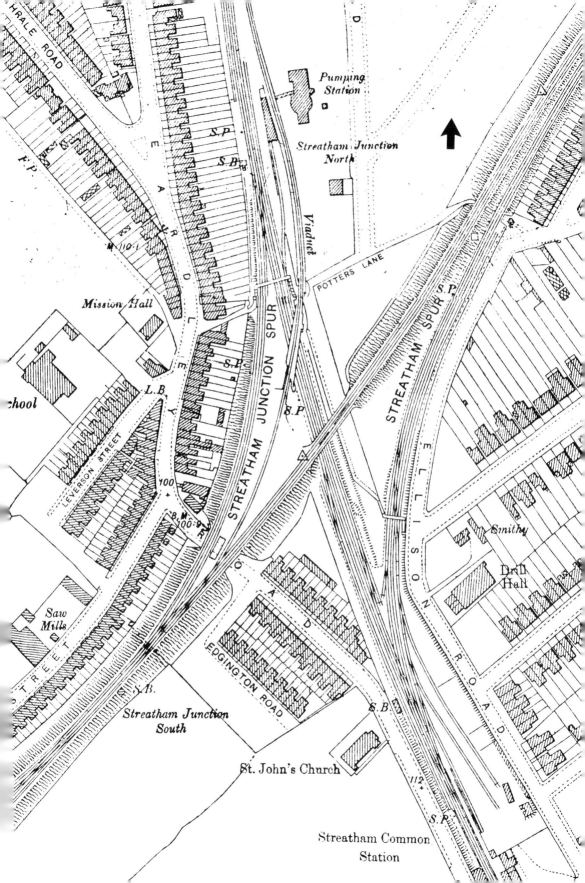

Pumping
Station

Streatham Junction
North

HALE ROAD

F.P.

S.P.

S.B.

M 110·1

Viaduct

POTTERS LANE

STREATHAM SPUR

S.P.

Mission Hall

m

S.P.

L.B.

LEVERSON STREET

STREATHAM JUNCTION SPUR

S.P.

S.P.

chool

100

B.M. 100·9

ELLISON ROAD

Smithy

Drill
Hall

Saw
Mills

STREET

EDGINGTON ROAD

S.B.

S.B.

Streatham Junction
South

St. John's Church

112

Streatham Common
Station

S.P.

76. The station was opened on 1st December 1862 but between 1st September 1868 and 1st January 1870 it was known as Greyhoundlane. It was rebuilt in 1900-03 in connection with the quadrupling of the lines to Selhurst. (Lens of Sutton)

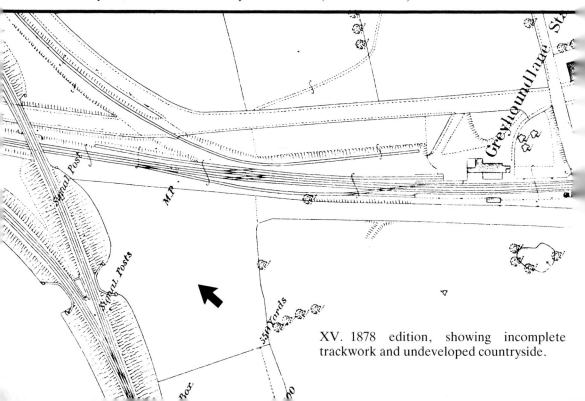

XV. 1878 edition, showing incomplete trackwork and undeveloped countryside.

77. In common with all the stations on this part of the route, it was rebuilt with platforms of very generous width. The last regular steam-hauled services originated from the Oxted line. Three aspect colour light signals were installed as far as Thornton Heath on 3rd February 1936. (Lens of Sutton)

78. In 1924, there was still open countryside in the vicinity of South Box, past which hurries class B4X no. 52 bound for East-bourne. Eleven goods sidings with four reception roads were provided south of the station, on the up side.
(S.C. Nash collection)

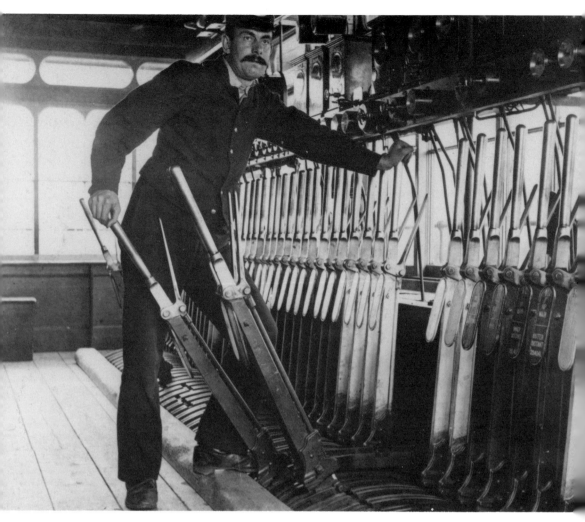

79. This is the interior of Streatham Common South Box, seen in the previous picture, which remained in use until 16th February 1936, when colour light signals were introduced. The North Box survived until 12th October 1952.
(D. Cullum collection)

CROYDON and CRYSTAL PALACE to KENSINGTON and VICTORIA.—Brighton and South Coast.

☞ **All 1,2,3 class,** unless otherwise stated.

Up. — **Week Days**—*Continued below.*

Up.	mrn	mrn	mrn	mrn	mrn	mrn	mrn	mrn	mrn	mrn	mrn	aft	aft	aft	aft	aft	aft	aft	aft	aft	aft	aft	aft	aft
Croydon(West)dp	7 10	8 3	...	9 10	...	9 37	...	1012	...	1120	...	...	1233	1 28	...	...	2 56	3 20	...	4 21	...	...	5 30	6 17
South Croydn ,,	...	...	...	...	9 11	...	10 3	...	...	...	1110	...	...	...	1 20	...	...	...	3 11	...	5 0	...	...	...
Centrl Croydn ,,	...	...	8 4	...	...	...	...	...	...	...	...	...	...	...	...	...	...	...	...	...	...	...	...	...
New Croydon..	...	...	8 14	...	9 16	...	10 8	...	...	...	1115	...	...	...	1 25	...	...	...	3 16	...	5 5	...	...	...
Norwood Junction	...	...	8 20	...	9 22	9 46	...	1018	...	...	1121	...	...	...	1 31	...	...	...	3 22	...	5 11	...	...	...
Crystal Palace ..	...	...	8 26	...	9 28	9 52	1017	1024	1037	...	1127	1236	...	...	1 37	2 1	...	...	3 28	...	5 17	5 33	...	...
Gipsy Hill	...	...	8 29	...	9 31	...	...	1027	...	...	1130	...	...	...	1 40	...	...	...	3 31	...	5 20	...	...	...
Lower Norwood ..	...	...	8 32	...	9 34	...	1022	1030	...	...	1133	...	...	...	1 43	...	...	...	3 34	...	5 23	...	...	...
Streatham Hill ..	...	...	8 37	...	9 39	10 0	1027	1035	1045	...	1138	1244	...	...	1 48	2 9	...	...	3 39	...	5 28	5 41	...	...
Selhurst	7 14	8 7	...	9 14	...	1&2 class only.	...	...	...	1124	...	...	1237	1 32	...	...	3 0	3 24	...	4 25	...	...	5 34	6 21
Thornton Heath	7 17	8 10	...	9 17	...		...	...	...	1127	...	...	1240	1 35	...	...	3 3	3 27	...	4 28	...	...	5 37	6 24
Greyhound Lane	7 22	8 15	...	9 22	...		...	...	...	1132	...	...	1245	1 40	...	...	3 8	3 32	...	4 33	...	...	5 42	6 29
Balham	7 28	8 21	8 40	9 28	9 42		...	1038	1048	1138	1141	...	1251	1 46	1 51	...	3 14	3 38	3 42	4 39	5 31	5 44	5 48	6 35
New Wandsworth	7 32	8 25	...	9 32	...		...	1042	...	...	1145	...	1255	...	1 55	...	...	...	...	4 43	...	...	5 52	...
Clapham J.32,40,	7 33	8 26	8 44	9 33	9 46	10 6	1033	1043	1052	1142	1146	1250	1256	1 50	1 56	2 15	3 18	3 42	3 46	4 44	5 35	5 48	5 53	6 39
W Lndn Battersea.. [46	7 53	...	8 54	...	9 58	1016	1044	...	1056	...	1154	1254	...	...	2 16	2 19	...	...	3 53	5 16	...	...	...	6 45
W Lndn Chelsea.... [28	7 56	...	8 57	...	9 56	1019	1047	...	1059	...	1157	1257	...	...	2 19	2 22	...	...	3 56	5 19	...	5 54	...	6 48
W Lndn W.Brmptn [24,	7 59	...	9 0	...	9 59	1022	1050	...	11 2	...	12 0	1 0	...	...	2 22	2 25	...	...	3 59	5 22	...	5 57	...	6 51
W Lndn Knsngtn 125,8	8 2	...	9 3	...	10 2	1025	1053	...	11 5	...	12 3	1 3	...	...	2 25	2 28	...	...	4 2	5 25	...	6 0	...	6 54
York Road	7 40	8 33	8 51	...	9 53	...	...	1050	...	1149	...	...	...	1 57	...	...	...	...	...	4 51	5 42	...	...	6 46
Battersea Park ..	7 42	...	8 53	...	...	...	...	1052	...	...	1154	...	1 4	...	...	...	3 26	...	...	...	...	...	...	6 48
Victoria......arr	7 45	8 37	8 56	9 42	9 57	1015	1042	1055	...	1153	1157	...	1 7	2 1	2 5	...	3 29	3 51	3 54	4 55	5 46	...	6 2	6 51

Up. — **Week Days**—*Continued.* / **Sundays.**

Up.	aft	aft	aft	aft	aft	aft	aft	aft	aft			Sun. mrn	mrn	aft	aft	aft	aft	aft	aft	aft	
Croydon (West)dp	...	...	...	7 38	...	8 28	9 33	...	1020	...	...	1034	...	2 25	4 19	...	7 0	7 39	8 45	1037	...
South Croydn ,,	...	...	...	...	7 58	...	...	9 47	...	...	...	...	...	...	...	...	...	...	...	...	...
Cntrl Croydon,,	6 16	...	7 34	...	...	...	...	...	...	...	...	...	1025	...	...	4 10	...	7 58	...	...	...
New Croydon..	6 21	...	7 39	...	8 8	...	...	9 52	...	...	...	...	1030	...	...	4 15	...	8 3	...	...	...
Norwood Junction	6 27	...	...	7 44	8 9	...	...	9 58	...	...	...	...	1036	...	...	4 21	...	8 9	...	...	...
Crystal Palace ..	6 33	7 5	...	7 50	8 15	...	...	10 4	...	...	...	...	1042	...	...	4 27	...	8 15	...	...	...
Gipsy Hill	6 36	...	...	7 53	8 18	...	...	10 7	...	...	...	...	1045	...	...	4 30	...	8 18	...	...	...
Lower Norwood ..	6 39	...	...	7 56	8 21	...	...	1010	...	...	...	...	1048	...	...	4 33	...	8 21	...	...	...
Streatham Hill ..	6 44	7 13	...	8 1	8 26	...	...	1015	...	...	...	...	1054	...	...	4 39	...	8 27	...	...	...
Selhurst	...	...	7 43	...	...	8 32	9 37	...	1024	...	...	1038	...	2 29	4 23	...	7 4	...	8 49	1041	...
Thornton Heath	...	...	7 46	...	...	8 35	9 40	...	1027	...	...	1041	...	2 32	4 26	...	7 7	...	8 52	1044	...
Greyhound Lane	...	...	7 51	...	...	8 40	9 45	...	1032	...	...	1046	...	2 37	4 31	...	7 12	...	8 57	1049	...
Balham	6 47	7 16	7 57	8 4	8 29	8 46	9 51	1018	1038	...	...	1052	1057	2 43	4 37	4 42	7 18	8 30	9 3	1055	...
New Wandsworth	6 51	...	8 1	8 8	8 33	8 50	9 55	1022	1042	...	...	1056	11 1	2 47	...	4 46	7 22	8 34	...	1059	...
Clapham J.32,40,	6 52	7 20	8 2	8 9	8 34	8 51	9 56	1023	1043	...	...	1057	11 2	2 48	4 41	4 47	7 23	8 35	9 7	11 0	...
W Lndn Battersea ..[46	...	...	...	8 18	8 46	...	1018	...	...	...	...	...	1118	3 15	...	4 58	7 38	...	9 15	...	...
W Lndn Chelsea ....[28	...	7 26	...	8 21	8 49	...	1021	...	...	...	...	...	1121	3 18	...	5 1	7 41	...	9 18	...	...
W Lndn W. Brmptn [24,	...	7 29	...	8 24	8 52	...	1024	...	...	...	...	...	1124	3 21	...	5 4	7 44	...	9 21	...	...
W Lndn Knsngtn 125,8,	...	7 32	...	8 28	8 55	...	1027	...	...	...	...	...	1127	3 24	...	5 7	7 47	...	9 24	...	...
York Road	...	...	8 9	8 16	...	...	10 3	...	...	...	...	...	1111	2 57	...	4 56	...	8 44	...	11 9	...
Battersea Park ..	...	...	8 11	...	...	8 59	...	1031	1051	...	...	11 7	...	2 59	...	4 58	7 33	8 46	9 17	...	...
Victoria ......arr	7 1	...	8 14	8 20	8 43	9 2	10 7	1034	1054	...	...	1110	1115	3 2	4 52	5 1	7 36	8 49	9 20	1113	...

☞ Passengers wishing to join the Main Line must change at New Croydon (adjoining East Croydon), Norwood Junction, or Clapham Junction.

VICTORIA and KENSINGTON to CRYSTAL PALACE and CROYDON.—Brighton and South Coast.

☞ **All 1,2,3 class,** unless otherwise stated.

Fares. / **Down.** — **Week Days**—*Continued below.*

Fares 1 cl. s. d.	2 cl. s. d.	3 cl. s. d.	Down.	mrn	mrn	mrn	mrn	mrn	mrn	mrn	mrn	mrn	mrn	aft	aft	aft	aft	aft	aft	aft	aft	aft	aft	aft
			Victoria,...dep	7 0	7 40	8 55	9 4	9 32	...	10 4	11 9	1130	...	1211	1 11	1 20	...	...	2 14	...	3 10	3 24	4 11	4 25
0 4	0 3	0 2	Battersea Park	7 4	...	...	...	...	...	...	1113	...	...	1215	1 13	1 24	...	...	...	...	...	3 28	4 15	...
0 4	0 3	0 2	York Road ...	...	...	...	...	9 37	...	10 9	1115	1135	...	1217	1 17	...	...	...	2 19	...	...	...	...	...
...	...	...	West London Knsngtn d	6 15	7 30	8 29	8 53	9 15	9 53	...	1053	1126	1153	1155	1253	...	1 25	1 53	...	2 57	...	...	3 53	...
0 5	0 4	0 3	West London W. Brmptn	6 18	7 33	8 32	8 56	9 18	9 56	...	1056	1129	12 1	1158	1256	...	...	1 56	...	...	...	...	3 56	...
0 6	0 4	0 3	West London Chelsea....	6 20	7 35	8 34	8 58	9 20	9 58	...	1058	1131	12 3	12 0	1258	...	1 29	1 58	...	3 1	...	...	3 58	...
0 6	0 4	0 3	West London Battersea..	6 23	7 38	8 37	9 1	9 23	10 1	...	11 1	1134	12 6	12 3	1 1	...	...	2 1	...	...	...	...	4 1	...
0 6	0 4	0 2	Clapham Junc.	7 10	7 48	9 3	9 12	9 42	10 5	1014	1120	1140	1211	1222	1 22	1 30	1 36	2 5	2 24	3 7	3 18	3 34	4 21	4 33
0 9	0 7	0 3	New Wndswrth	7 12	...	...	...	...	...	...	1122	...	...	1224	1 24	...	...	...	...	...	...	...	4 23	4 35
0 11	0 9	0 4	Balham,.......	7 17	7 53	9 8	9 17	9 47	1010	1019	1127	1145	1216	1229	1 29	1 35	1 41	...	2 29	3 12	3 23	3 39	4 28	4 40
1 3	1 0	0 6	Greyhound L.	7 22	...	9 13	...	...	...	...	1132	...	...	1234	1 34	...	...	...	2 34	...	3 28	...	4 33	...
1 3	1 0	0 7	Thornton Hth	7 27	...	9 18	...	...	...	...	1137	...	...	1239	1 39	...	...	...	2 39	...	3 33	...	4 38	...
1 3	1 0	0 7	Selhurst	7 30	...	9 21	...	...	...	...	1140	...	...	1242	1 42	...	...	...	2 42	...	3 36	...	4 41	...
1 2	0 11	0 5	Streatham Hill.	...	7 57	...	9 21	9 51	1014	1023	...	1149	1220	...	...	1 39	1 45	2 12	...	3 16	...	3 43	...	4 44
1 3	1 0	0 6	Lower Norwood	...	8 1	...	9 25	9 55	...	1027	...	...	...	...	...	1 43	1 49	...	...	...	...	3 47	...	4 48
1 3	1 0	0 7	Gipsy Hill ...	...	...	...	...	9 59	...	1031	...	...	...	...	...	1 47	...	...	...	...	...	3 51	...	4 52
1 3	1 0	0 7	Crystal Palace	...	8 8	...	9 32	10 3	1022	1035	...	1159	1228	...	...	1 51	1 55	2 20	...	3 24	...	3 55	...	4 56
1 3	1 0	0 8	Norwood Jn. 48	...	8 12	...	9 36	10 7	...	1039	...	12 3	...	...	...	1 55	...	Sats. only.	...	...	...	3 59	...	5 0
1 6	1 2	0 10	Nw Croydn 48	...	8 18	...	9 42	...	...	1045	...	12 9	...	...	...	2 1	...		...	...	...	4 5	...	5 6
1 6	1 2	0 10	Cen. Croydon a	...	...	...	...	...	...	...	...	...	...	...	...	...	...		...	...	...	[illegible]	...	5 9
1 6	1 2	0 10	Sth Croydon ,,	...	8 21	...	9 45	...	...	1048	...	1212	...	...	...	2 4	...		...	...	...	4 8	...	...
1 6	1 2	0 10	Croydn (West),,	7 33	...	9 24	...	1011	...	...	1143	...	...	1245	1 45	...	...		2 45	...	2 39	...	4 44	...

Down. — **Week Days**—*Continued.* / **Sundays.**

Down.	aft	aft	aft	aft	aft	aft	aft	aft	aft	aft	aft	ngt.			Sun. mrn	mrn	aft	aft	aft	aft	aft	aft	aft	aft
Victoria ....dep	4 46	5 14	5 28	6 0	6 18	...	7 9	7 45	8 1	8 57	10 8	12 5	...	...	6 30	9 3	1239	1 0	3 20	3 30	5 15	5 30	7 53	9 50
Battersea Park ..	1&2 class only.	5 18	1&2 class only.	...	...	...	7 13	7 49	8 5	...	...	...	...	...	6 34	9 7	1243	1 4	3 24	3 34	...	5 34	7 57	9 54
York Road		...		...	...	...	7 15	7 51	8 7	9 2	10 8	1210	...	...	...	...	1245	1 6	...	3 36	5 20	...	7 59	...
West London Kensingtn d		...		5 53	...	6 15	6 55	7 18	7 53	8 53	9 46	...	...	...	...	...	...	...	2 50	...	...	5 22	...	9 30
West London WstBrmptn		...		5 56	...	6 18	6 58	7 21	7 56	8 56	9 49	...	...	...	...	...	...	...	2 53	...	...	5 25	...	9 33
West London Chelsea		...		5 58	...	6 20	7 0	7 23	7 58	8 58	9 51	...	...	...	...	...	...	...	2 56	...	...	5 28	...	9 36
West London Battersea ..		...		6 1	...	6 22	7 3	7 26	8 1	9 1	9 54	...	...	...	...	...	...	...	2 59	...	...	5 31	...	9 39
Clapham Junc..		5 24		6 8	6 26	6 27	7 20	7 56	8 12	9 7	1013	1215	...	...	6 40	9 13	1250	1 11	3 30	3 41	5 25	5 40	8 4	10 0
New Wandswrth		...		6 10	...	...	7 22	...	8 14	...	1015	1217	...	...	6 42	9 15	1252	1 13	3 32	3 43	5 27	5 42	8 6	10 2
Balham		5 29		6 15	6 31	6 32	7 27	8 1	8 19	9 12	1020	1222	...	...	6 47	9 20	1257	1 18	3 37	3 48	5 32	5 47	8 11	10 7
Greyhound Lne		...		...	6 36	...	7 32	8 6	...	...	...	...	...	...	...	9 25	...	1 23	3 42	...	...	5 52	8 16	1012
Thornton Hth.		...		...	6 41	...	7 37	8 11	...	...	...	...	...	...	...	9 30	...	1 28	3 47	...	...	5 57	8 21	1017
Selhurst		...		...	6 44	...	7 40	8 14	...	...	...	...	...	...	...	9 33	...	1 31	3 50	...	...	6 0	8 24	1020
Streatham Hill..	4 49	5 33	5 41	6 19	...	6 36	...	...	8 23	9 16	1024	1226	...	...	6 51	...	1 1	...	...	3 52	5 36	...	...	...
Lower Norwood	...	5 37	...	6 23	...	6 40	...	...	8 27	9 20	1028	1230	...	...	6 55	...	1 5	...	...	3 56	5 40	...	...	...
Gipsy Hill......	...	5 41	...	6 27	...	6 44	...	...	8 31	...	1032	1234	...	...	7 0	...	1 10	...	...	4 1	5 45	...	...	...
Crystal Palace	5 9	5 45	5 51	6 31	...	6 46	...	...	8 35	9 27	1036	1238	...	...	7 5	...	1 15	...	...	4 15	5 50	...	...	...
Norwood Jnc. 48	5 13	5 49	5 55	6 35	...	...	...	...	8 39	9 31	1040	1242	...	...	7 9	...	1 19	...	...	4 19	5 54	...	...	...
New Crydn 48	...	5 55	...	6 41	...	...	...	8 19	...	9 37	...	...	...	...	7 15	...	1 25	...	...	...	6 0	...	...	...
Cen. Croydn a	...	5 58	...	...	...	...	...	...	...	...	...	...	...	...	7 18	...	1 28	...	...	...	6 3	...	...	...
Sth. Croydn. ,,	...	...	...	6 44	...	...	...	8 22	...	9 40	...	...	...	...	...	...	...	...	...	...	...	...	...	...
Croydon(West),,	5 17	...	5 59	...	6 47	...	7 43	...	8 43	...	1044	1246	...	...	...	9 36	...	1 34	3 53	4 23	...	6 3	8 27	1023

Bradshaw 1869.

NORBURY

80. The station was built speculatively in conjunction with local estate developers who paid one third of its cost. It is situated at the south end of Streatham High Road and opened in January 1878. (Lens of Sutton)

XVI. 1913.

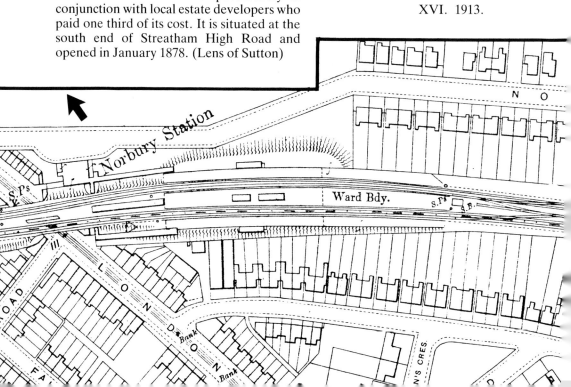

81. Another southbound train speeds through, this time hauled by U1 class no. 1902, devoid of the more familiar smoke deflectors. The massive canopies amplified the sounds of a passing locomotive most memorably. (D. Cullum collection)

82. Circular windows appear in the design of most of the contemporary stations on the line and help to give the desired impression of importance. The Ford 8 and Standard 10 are reminders of a later era – the 1930s. (Lens of Sutton)

83. At 11.30am on 29th October 1940, enemy action resulted in the partial destruction of the approach to the island platform. The line was not unfamiliar with aerial attack – Streatham Common station and shunting box had been hit by bombs in September 1916. (British Rail)

84. A 1968 photograph reveals that the approach to the down local platform had to be entirely rebuilt as a result of wartime destruction. The main line platforms, on the right, are now only used in an emergency. (British Rail)

London Brighton & South Coast Rᴸʸ

3RD CLASS (LIMITED) PULLMAN EXPRESS

BETWEEN

LONDON & BRIGHTON

EVERY SUNDAY

DOWN.		a.m.	UP.		p.m.
VICTORIA	... dep.	9.45	BRIGHTON	... dep.	6.35
Clapham Jct. ...	,,	9.52	East Croydon ...	arr.	7.21
East Croydon ...	,,	10. 6	Clapham Jct. ...	,,	7.36
BRIGHTON	... arr.	10.54	VICTORIA	... ,,	7.44

Day Return Fare to Brighton—

From VICTORIA - - - 12/6

,, Clapham Junction - 12/0

,, East Croydon - - 10/6

The tickets are available by the above-mentioned trains and on the day of issue only.

Commencing October 8th this Train will also make additional (non-stop) runs as follows:—

UP.		a.m.	DOWN.		p.m.
BRIGHTON	dep.	11.30	VICTORIA	dep.	4.55
VICTORIA	arr.	p.m. 12.35	BRIGHTON	arr.	6. 0

Ordinary 3rd Class fares (plus Pullman Car supplement) will be charged on these trips.

The number of seats is strictly limited.

Refreshments are obtainable on the train.

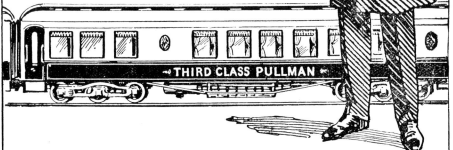

WILLIAM FORBES,
General Manager

LONDON BRIDGE TERMINUS

THORNTON HEATH

85. The station opened with the line and was rebuilt with the others in 1900-03. Top people arrive in their top hats whilst the station is topped by a cupola. Typical local road transport of the day is on show, the tramcar being one of the rival Croydon Corporation Tramways. (Lens of Sutton)

XVII. 1877.

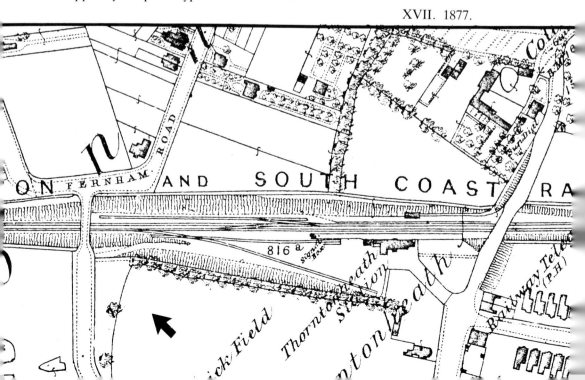

86. The signal box is at the end of the down platform, whereas the 1877 map shows one on the up platform. It is of an early design, of which a rare example survived in 1987 at Billingshurst and is shown in picture no. 63 in our *Crawley to Littlehampton* album. (Lens of Sutton)

XVIII. 1913.

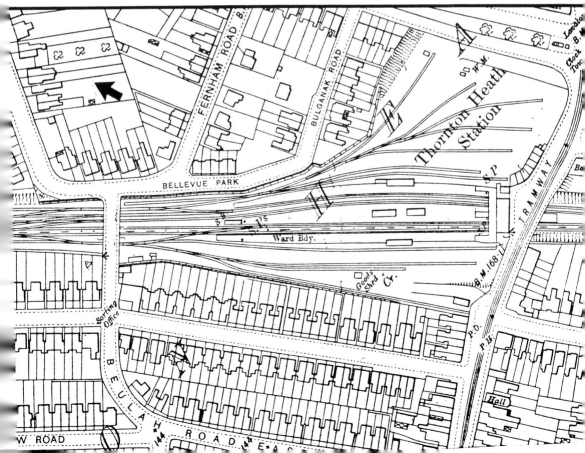

87. The interior in 1897 contained a Saxby &
Farmer lever frame with Sykes Lock & Block
instruments. (P.J. Mullett/P. Hay collection)

88. The signalman's view of the station included the goods yard on the right, which contained a small goods shed. Look at the height of the signals. (Lens of Sutton)

89. The booking office was still gas lit when photographed in October 1949. With £.s.d. and innumerable different card tickets, the balancing of the books at the end of a shift could be difficult. (British Rail)

90. A fan of seven sidings for coal traffic was provided on the down side. It was not unusual for coal to be segregated from general merchandise but it was usually for geographical reasons. (Lens of Sutton)

91. The 13.36 Victoria to Horsham service passes under Brook Road bridge on 8th August 1969. After 1952, the signal box was only manned during shunting operations. (J. Scrace)

92. A photograph from August 1986 shows that the fine architectural details have been largely retained and that passengers now benefit from modern train indicators and, indeed, trains. The back of the train indicates where it has come from. (A.C. Mott)

93. This is the view south, before the lines were widened to Balham, showing the station which was opened on 1st May 1865, nearly 2½ years after the line. (Lens of Sutton)

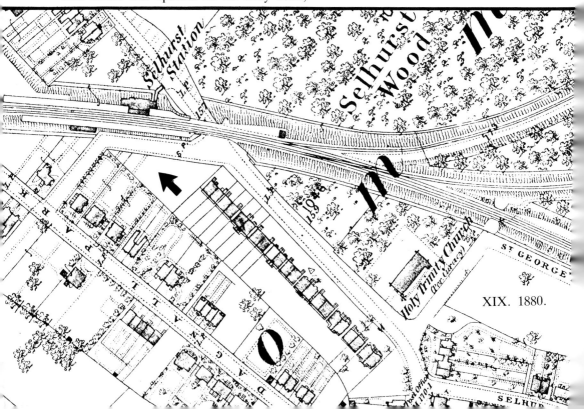

94. The up platform was of similar timber construction, the overall appearance being that of a rural station, in keeping with the contemporary surroundings. (Lens of Sutton)

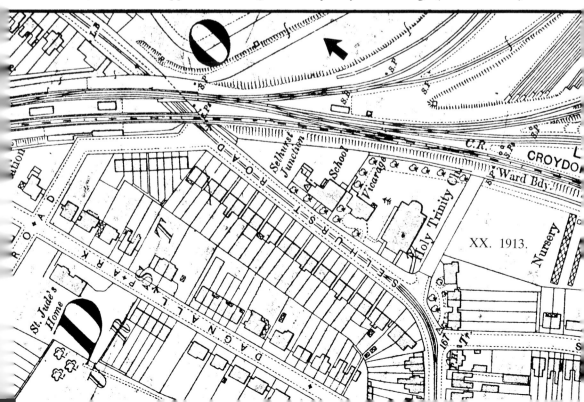

95. Selhurst Junction box appears complete as work proceeds on the rearrangement of the trackwork prior to the introduction of four-track working to Balham . (Lens of Sutton)

96. The urban development of the area proceeded apace and a spacious station was provided after the quadrupling was completed in 1903. (Lens of Sutton)

97. New signals are finished off as the additional tracks stand ready for use. The distant signals are fitted with Coligny-Welch illuminated fishtails, neither the arms or the lamp glasses being yellow at that time. (Lens of Sutton)

98. In 1954, the station retained its gaslights and its unusual crossover between the platforms. In common with all the stations north, it has lost the canopy from the single up main platform, seen on the left. (D. Cullum)

99. Colour light signals came into use between here and East Croydon on 21st March 1954. This is the scene two weeks before and shows the lines to the carriage depot branching to the left and the main lines curving away to the right. (D. Cullum)

100. Selhurst Depot has been expanded to become the major maintenance facility for the former Central Division's electric rolling stock. Routine examinations, general overhauls, painting and interior renovation are undertaken in a series of three massive sheds. (A.C. Mott)

101. The old Gloucester Road Junction signal box was superseded by the 131-lever box on the left, in March 1954. The lines from West Croydon are on the left and those from East Croydon are on the right and in the foreground. (D. Cullum)

London Brighton and South Coast Railway

Crowborough to

Selhurst

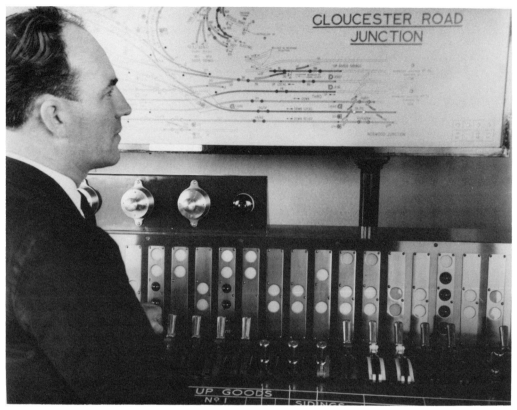

102. Electric switches or push-buttons could have been used but signalmen were reluctant to be parted from their traditional levers and so miniature ones were installed for many years, this box having 38.
(D. Cullum collection)

XXI. 1949 signal diagram. (Railway Magazine)

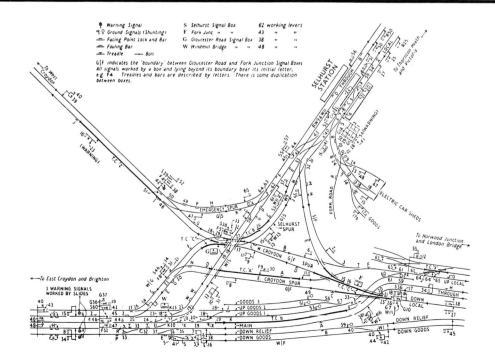

103. Windmill Bridge Junction Box and its up signal bridge as seen in 1907. The three ringed arms were for 'Teetotal' sidings, which were parallel to the London Bridge lines. They were reputed to be the furthest possible from a pub. (Lens of Sutton)

104. Looking south in 1954, we see Windmill Bridge Junction Box in the distance and the old position of the convergence of the Victoria and London Bridge local lines on the right. During the remodelling of the junctions in 1983, hundreds of tons of waste from Betteshanger Colliery were unloaded on the spare land on the left. This gave rise to rumours of coal stockpiling in anticipation of the next miners strike. (D. Cullum)

EAST CROYDON

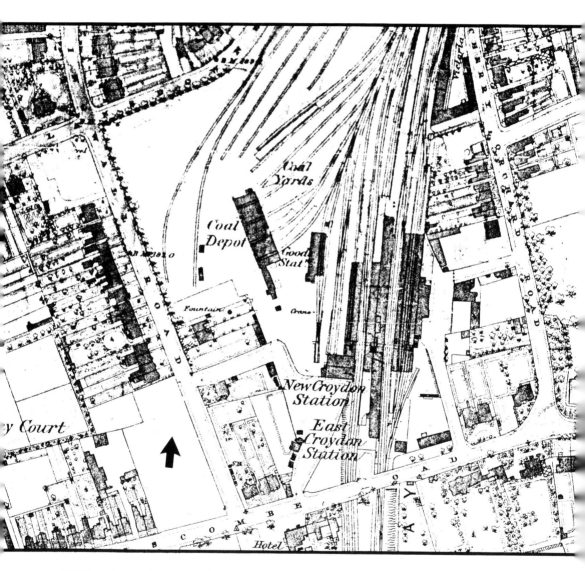

XXII. The station came into use with the opening of the line between Norwood and Haywards Heath on 12th July 1841. Separate local lines from Windmill Bridge Junction were provided on 1st May 1862 to an adjacent but independent station, known as New Croydon. This 1866 map shows the separate road approaches to both stations on either side of the railway. The additional double track had been extended southward on 1st September 1865, to South Croydon. In 1868, a branch from it was opened to Central Croydon, a terminus close to the High Street, adjacent to Katherine Street. The main lines were shared by the LBSCR and the SER.

105. The down express on the then main line is headed by a class B2 4–4–0, in about 1904. The name New Croydon was dropped in 1909, the eastern part of the station subsequently being known as East Croydon Local. (Lens of Sutton)

106. An Edwardian view of the exterior shows the 1894 building which is little changed today and now has to cope with double commuter traffic each morning – local residents leaving for London and people arriving to work in the lofty office blocks that have sprouted up in the area in recent years. There are many architectural features in common with the SER station at Tunbridge Wells. (Lens of Sutton)

107. One of the District Engineer's inspection cars was kept at East Croydon and was photographed there in 1906. The LBSCR was noted for innovation! The controls and horn appear to be for a back-seat driver. (E.R. Lacey collection)

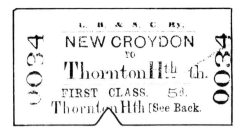

108. The builders' merchant Hall & Co had sidings on the east side of the line and shunted them with this Clayton & Shuttleworth traction engine apparentlyt mounted on a wagon underframe. Look for the balls of the governor and the chain tensioner. (Lens of Sutton)

109. The station still consists of three island platforms, this being a northward view between the western two, prior to electrification. It shows the down local lines and the up loop. The boundary between 'New' and 'East' had been where the central track is situated. (Lens of Sutton)

110. Moving east along the footbridge, we look down on platforms 4 and 5 and see North Box in the distance. The ramps to the platforms are used by passengers to perform amazing athletic feats, aided by gravity. Up trains used to divide here to the two London termini and as late as 1924, two 'Terriers' could be seen barking away with a London Bridge portion. (Lens of Sutton)

111. Looking north from North Box in July 1923, the goods yard is visible on the left and the Victoria Wharf of Hall & Co on the right. The size of the locomotive water tank reflects the extent of the steam operation in those days. (Late E. Wallis)

112. Looking out from the other end of the box, it is interesting to note that the middle siding, between platforms 2 and 3, had its own loop. This was no doubt useful for the station pilot, when shunting horse boxes and vans of perishables from one passenger train to another. It also had a locomotive inspection pit. (Late E. Wallis)

XXIII. Rearrangement of the lines through East Croydon was completed in October 1983. All fast trains would use platforms 1, 2 and 3 and the number of crossings of trains on the level reduced by the greater use of fly-overs. The old arrangement is shown at the top. (Railway Magazine)

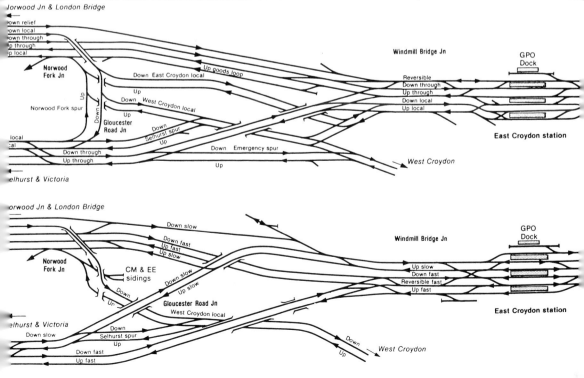

113. The advent of electric trains in 1925 helped speed the flow of passengers. Traffic of local origin alone increased enormously as the population rose from 13,000 in 1841 to 190,000 in 1921. The signals are the Up Loop starters. (Lens of Sutton)

114. The east side of the station has for long been associated with postal traffic. The dock for this traffic was unusual in having a cross-over in such a short siding. Two items now almost extinct on BR are the loading gauge and water crane. (Lens of Sutton)

115. The through *passenger* service to the LMS ceased prior to WWII but it continued to operate for goods and is seen here with a cattle truck and a CWS milk tanker. This efficient form of road/rail transport was not further developed, regrettably, but has recently been re-invented for use in the Channel Tunnel and will hopefully be used further inland. (Lens of Sutton)

goods yard was closed in May 1973 and the goods shed demolished in 1986. There is now seldom a quiet moment at this interesting and remunerative traffic centre. (J. Scrace)

117. The 11.08 Victoria to Eastbourne via Heathfield passes under the signal bridge on 10th October 1953 and is composed of ageing 'Birdcage' coaches. The semaphore signals were abandoned on 21st March 1954 in favour of colour lights which could give a mere 2½ minute headway between trains. (S.C. Nash)

118. A sign of change as no. E5018 pilots no. 73115 *King Pellimore* at the head of 9.31 Victoria to Newhaven Harbour boat train on 9th April 1964. Currently one Newhaven service is extended to start at Manchester, giving East Croydon three through trains a day to that city. (S.C. Nash)

119. A 1968 photograph shows the former coal yard to be occupied by road vans but the goods yard to be still well used. The gantry crane, seen near the signal box, was of 10-ton capacity. (E. Wilmshurst)

120. No. 73123 hauls a special inaugural train on 10th May 1984. The traffic pattern changed dramatically on that day, with the introduction of a 15-minute interval service to Gatwick Airport, although not stopping at East Croydon. Nevertheless, the station has an excellent direct service to all towns between Hastings and Portsmouth with all fast trains to Brighton now stopping. (J. Scrace)

Easebourne Lane, Midhurst, West Sussex. GU29 9AZ Tel: 01730 813169 Fax: 01730 812601
. . . WRITE OR PHONE FOR OUR LATEST LIST . . .